Courage in the Face of Experts

Adventures Off The Road Most Traveled

by Kelli Swan

Courage in the Face of Experts
Adventures Off The Road Most Traveled
Copyright © 2022 Kelli S. Swan

Writing, editing, and spot illustrations by Kelli Swan

Cover artwork by Terry Paczko
www.terrypaczko.com
A professional illustrator, Terry Paczko is a master of the art of visual communication. His creative images have solved client messaging challenges that only the most unique visuals can address.

Kelli Swan, Publisher
Author/Publisher website:
www.kelliswan.com

ISBN 978-1-387-36878-5

A Few Favorites

Avoiding danger is no safer in the long run than outright exposure. Life is either a daring adventure or nothing.

~ Helen Keller

The intellect has little to do on the road to discovery. There comes a leap in consciousness, call it intuition or what you will, and the solution comes to you and you don't know how or why.

~ Albert Einstein

Trust in the Lord with all your heart and lean not on your own understanding

~ Proverb: 3:5(NIV)

You learn to speak by speaking, to study by studying, to run by running, to work by working; and just so you learn to love God and man by loving. Begin as a mere apprentice and the very power of love will lead you on to become a master of the art.

~ Saint Francis De Sales

It's not that the Bible is true. It's that the Bible is the prerequisite for the manifestation of truth, which makes it far more true than just 'true.' It's a whole different kind of truth. And I think that's not just literally the case – in fact – I think it can't be otherwise. This is the only way to solve the problem of perception.

~ Dr. Jordan B. Peterson

Contents

ME

HORSES

DOGS

Final Thoughts

Courage in the Face of Experts
Adventures Off The Road Most Traveled

Enclosed within this book are a few stories about my journey of learning to trust faith and inner wisdom over logic and experts ... stories about discovering health and hope through unconventional channels.

"For we walk by faith, not by sight." ~ 2 Corinthians 5:7

Introduction

On the following pages you will find a number of true accounts from my personal journey of learning to trust my **inner guidance**. These are stories of grace. Or magic. Or crazy-ass coincidences. Call it what you like. For me, these events have been defined by listening to, and acting on (or not acting on), guidance from beyond my rational understanding.

My journey has largely been about learning to **trust** this guidance with increasing confidence as I age. Along with trusting the subsequent *other* lessons, like how to be courageous in the face of *experts* who demand that I ignore my inner guidance, and follow *their* advice.

Intuition, inner guidance, the inner voice ... I'm not sure what else to call it. This guidance seems to know everything. It definitely knows far more than any *expert*. Yet I only see or hear the tiny pieces of knowledge and/or guidance that I can absorb at the moment it is needed. I generally refer to this knowing as *God*, or the *Realm of the Divine*.

Over the years, I've shared some of these stories verbally with friends and family. Often the response was *"Wow! Did that really happen?"* And occasionally, a story would launch a discussion about what it means to live one's truth ... to not fall prey to the assumption that the material world is all there is to life and that all answers can be found through reason. Those spirited conversations are nearly always my favorites.

My inspiration for writing this book was simply that I didn't want these stories to die with me. Perhaps one or more of my experiences might help or inspire another? Or not. I just know that I needed to create a record of these events.

And while Inner Guidance is applicable to just about any topic, most of the stories here represent the health-related experiences in my life. My cumulative takeaway from these experiences is that the most important aspect of living a healthy life, is *believing* that health is possible, that health is our natural state.

We were designed as self-balancing and self-healing organisms. For the most part, *health* means learning to support that design, not trying to change it or micromanage it. Once the belief in the possibility of health-by-design is acknowledged, one can be led to all sorts of alternative approaches that were previously invisible.

Part of my greater journey has been the deep contemplation of my own mortality. It was only when I allowed myself to fully accept that this time on earth is temporary that my life began to take on new levels of health and meaning.

The stories in this book are written in more or less chronological order, so you might notice a bit of an evolution in how I've interpreted the events that took place. Like anything else, as one gains experiential knowledge on a path, one tends to become more confident of the decisions on that path.

Disclaimers and Exceptions

Some of these stories will sound too bizarre to be true. I promise you, each and every story in this book actually happened. Mostly as I have presented them here, however minor liberties were taken to shorten the tales into something easily digestible. I generally like to think of myself as a *creative* person, but even I am not creative enough to make this stuff up!

The names and roles of people in these stories have been changed and made as generic as possible. I've mostly ommitted locations as well. It's not my intention to point fingers at anyone. Again, I'm just sharing my experiences. The pet's names remain unchanged, as of course, animals don't have reputations, egos, or livelihoods to protect.

And I want to acknowledge the **many** great doctors and veterinarians out there, those who have not completely sold out to Rockefeller Medicine. I have been blessed to know quite a few wonderful professionals through the years. These stories are in no way meant to demean any particular person or profession. Nearly everyone in those professions has honorable intentions. They have to work within systems that have been corrupted by both good intentions and malevolent ones as well. It is unfortunate that we humans have developed a healthcare system for ourselves and our pets that relies on *creating customers*. As such, there is little incentive to keep customers healthy, happy, and *not* in need of services. A steady stream of repeat business is required to support and grow the systems. And as far as I can tell, mainstream healthcare really excels at *that*.

These stories intentionally run light on technical lingo. Thus, you may find my terminology lacking in places. I have made no attempts to make this a scientific deep-dive. I hope you enjoy the conversational approach, and ideas herein.

ME

Fourteen, Fat, and Fed Up
My First Experience of The Inner Voice

As an introvert and a typically emotional teen, I used food as my go-to for just about everything. Happy? Celebrate with food. Sad? Drown sorrows with food. Unsure of myself? Decide on next snack and problem solved. And so on. By fourteen years of age I weighed over 175 pounds, and was gaining fast.

As far as school social demographics went, an overweight redheaded girl who had good grades was pretty low on the acceptance scale. I was terrible at most sports, so was always one of the last team members to be picked by team captains. Of course kids didn't realize the damage they did when they made fun of other kids, so the ridicule was frequent. School, and after school events, were often unpleasant experiences. (I thank God all this took place before social media and smart phones!)

I recall Thanksgiving dinner the year I turned fourteen. I was stressed out by yet another holiday with too many people around and too much drama. Food, as usual, became the solution. That day, I recall eating *two* entire thanksgiving meals. Two *full* plates, dessert and all.

Afterwards, I felt just miserable. I was wearing my largest pair of pants, and they had become so tight I could barely breath. I recall going to my room and looking at the reflection in the mirror, and not recognizing what I saw. It was as if someone else was looking back at me.

Next, a strange quiet came over me. I stood there, in a sort of trance, then heard a *voice* in my head. I say *voice* as I'm not sure what else to call it. They weren't words really, but a message just the same.

As I gazed at the reflection in the mirror, an Inner Voice said: *"That's not who I am."*

Then, all I remember was quiet.

I went to sleep that night, and slept peacefully. The next morning, it was as if a switch had flipped inside of me. I was to become something else … though I wasn't sure *what else* at the time. A single-minded focus was about to unfold.

That same day, I got on my bicycle, and rode two miles to the local A&P grocery store. Back then, stores sold little pocket paperbacks in the checkout area. I picked out two booklets and purchased them, at 50 cents a piece. One was a how-to booklet about dieting, and the other had lists of the calorie counts for common foods.

I read the dieting booklet as soon as I got home. It was a general overview about how to count calories and burn calories.

Upon finishing the books, my journey took off. I began calorie restriction to 1200 calories a day, and started doing every exercise I could think of. Some exercises I found in library books, or on television. Others were more obvious, like walking and riding my bike. Over the course of the next year I lost nearly 50 pounds. I became much more physically active, and interested in building both my mental and physical health. During that time, my dedication never wavered, not once. I just had this *something else* concept lodged inside.

I share the story quite humbly, and truly hope it does not sound like any sort of brag. Where a fourteen-year old could suddenly gets such inspiration and guidance is beyond me. It must have come from beyond the *self*. This was my earliest (remembered) experience of a knowingness that expressed itself in my life.

This transition was a life-changing process for me in many ways, as there was no *try to do it* involved. It was more like a pre-existing truth that I simply moved towards. That probably makes little sense, but I don't know how else to explain it. I think *trying* implies thoughts of potential failure, and I never experienced those thoughts.

My Takeaways: There is a world of difference between *trying* to do something while fretting about not doing it, and simply doing something. Sometimes inspiration happen by *grace*. Meaning, I don't believe my 14-year old self had the emotional competencies to just decide to figure out how to lose weight. I certainly wouldn't have possessed any amount of willpower that would have made a difference. The directional shift from within came from somewhere else. I can only credit divine guidance.

16

UTI's, IC, Pain, and more Pain

Experts Know What They Know
(and that's all some of them want to know)

During my late teens and early 20's, I struggled with frequent urinary tract infections (UTI's). For those who have never had a UTI, lucky you. For those who have had them, you know how painful these events can be. Imagine having acid in your bladder and then having to pass it.

By my mid 20's I was getting these infections so frequently that my doctor prescribed *refillable* antibiotics. This is unheard of today, but at the time, they didn't know what else to do for me. After years of this approach I was finally referred to a specialist.

The specialist (a urologist) decided that, at the first sign of an infection, I would need to go to a lab and provide a urine sample, so they could start culturing the bacteria and prescribe *better* antibiotics. (This is somewhat standard today, but again, back then the culturing of samples was reserved for more problematic cases.) This *test and prescribe* cycle went on for the next several rounds of UTI's, until one round when the doctor's office called and revealed that the latest culture had indicated that there was **no infection** present.

"Then why am I in pain?!" I asked. This episode resulted in another visit to the urologist, at which point I was informed that they wanted to do additional testing, to get to the root of the problem. This additional testing included a bladder biopsy which was performed as an outpatient procedure at a hospital.

The biopsy test results after this procedure resulted in an actual diagnosis: interstitial cystitis (IC), or chronic inflammation of the bladder.

For some reason, the lining of my bladder was chronically inflamed, and bleeding. The doctor theorized that this was allowing bacteria to invade and cause the infections. That was in addition to the ongoing pain from the inflammation itself.

After announcing the diagnosis, the doctor got to the fun part: this condition had no know cause, no known cure, and the only treatment available was considered experimental.

"Great ... wonderful," I thought. *"And what would that treatment be?"* I asked.

"We will instill 50 cc of DMSO into your bladder, once a week for 6 weeks in a row," he said. And he said this with a straight face.

Inner Voice: *"Wait. What?! That is barbaric, insane."*

A bit of background is needed here: I owned horses at that time, and was quite familiar with the use of dimethyl sulfoxide, or DMSO. Horse owners and trainers used DMSO topically as a liniment on horses legs It also had a reputation for helping with arthritis pain when used topically. Emphasis here on ***topically***, as in external, as in ***outside*** the body. DMSO was first discovered and used in the 1800's – it was an ***industrial solvent***. And this doctor planned on putting a catheter in me and inserting the liquid **inside** my body. (Seriously, who thinks of this stuff?!)

Absent a better plan, or any other direction to head, I finally decided to go ahead with the six experimental treatments. My first session took place on a Friday afternoon. The doctor inserted the catheter and proceeded to plunge the entire contents of a giant syringe into my bladder. I was then told to hold it for 1.5 hours, before going to the bathroom.

When I went to stand up, in preparation to leave the office, the pain from the DMSO on already inflamed tissue nearly caused me to pass out. I made it to my car, then nearly wrecked my vehicle on several occasions driving home. When I did arrive home, I called the doctor's office and screamed at them. *"Why didn't you warn me how painful this would be??"* They nonchalantly replied that I could take some ibuprofen and other pain medications an hour before the next treatment. *"(Geee, now you tell me. Thanks.")*

I made it through the next 5 weeks of treatments. Barely. For a short period of time, a few weeks in fact, I had hopes that the treatments had worked. Unfortunately, less than two months later, the same pain that had become routine prior to the DMSO treatments returned in full force. So, living through the painful treatment process had been all for nothing.

Well, not *nothing* entirely. A bunch of people made money on it, so there's that. (As a side note, it is my understanding that this *treatment* is now *FDA-approved.* Go figure.)

Time went on, and I just adapted to the recurring pain. I kept pain-killer drugs with me at all times. Sometimes I developed a full-blown UTI as well, so periodic lab runs, cultures, and antibiotics were also part of the fun. This cycle became my life.

A few years later, I was having lunch with someone who at the time was taking a master's level chemistry course. He related how he'd learned in his recent chemistry class that aspartame (an artificial sweetener) combines with nitrates (a preservative in things like hot dogs) in the body, and turns into the #1 brain carcinogen. Yuck!!! I already knew that I drank too much diet soda, and that soda wasn't good for the teeth. So here was another reason to ditch sodas and start drinking more water.

*Inner Voice: "Stop using aspartame, **immediately.**"*

So, I quite artificial sweeteners, cold turkey. Not only did I eliminate the diet sodas, I got rid of the diet jello, cookies, etc. All the diet products that I had come to live on (by mistakenly equating fewer calories with healthy eating) got dumped.

About 5 months went by, and one day it occurred to me that hadn't needed any pain medications recently. And strangely enough, while I did notice this, I didn't give it much more thought at the time.

Then, one night I awoke around 2:00 in the morning with *searing* bladder pain. It was very sudden, and very painful.

"WTH?!" I thought. *"This **can't** be a UTI – they don't come on this fast. This **has** to be something I ate."*

Upon further investigation, I discovered that the liquid flu "medication" that I'd taken the night before was sweetened with *aspartame.*

Bells rang, whistles blew. This time I *did* think about it. This time I *knew* the source of my bladder pain, beyond a shadow of a doubt. From then on, I was careful to read all labels when purchasing food, drink, or supplements – avoiding anything that contained aspartame. After that, I remained pain-free.

About six months later, I had a followup appointment with my urologist. And the following exchange took place.

Dr.: *How are you doing?*

Me: *Great! I figured out what was causing the interstitial cystitis.*

Dr.: *Huh?*

Me: *It was aspartame sweetener. Nutrasweet.*

Dr.: *Huh?*

Me: *I got the artificial sweeteners out of my diet, and I've been pain-free ever since.*

Dr.: *Oh.*

That's it – that was the entirety of our conversation in a nutshell. The nice doctor did a 180-degree turn on one heel, and headed out of the room. No other comment or questions. Nadda. Crickets.

I was dumbfounded. This guy ***knew*** how many years I'd struggled with this pain. Why did he not show the ***slightest*** bit of interest when I told him I felt better?!

My takeaways: Some doctors aren't interested in simple solutions that work (which would negate the need for a doctor.) Evidently they need jobs too. This doctor was a nice guy – very likable. I'm sure he meant no harm or disrespect. But to have a patient, one you know has struggled for years, suddenly show up in your office, vibrant and well, and ***not be the least bit interested*** in ***that***?!

A Kyro-What?

My Introduction to Alternative Medicine

I was in my mid 30's and spending long hours at both a computer and a drawing table. After many, many hours of this, I began experiencing an increasingly stiff neck, with occasional mild pain. I didn't give this too much thought, until I went to a hair stylist one day for a hair shampoo and cut, and found that I couldn't flex my head back into the wash tub rest. "*That's weird,*" I thought. We worked around it, I got my hair cut, and my thoughts quickly moved on to other things. I didn't think it was that significant.

A few days later, I awoke to sharp pain in my left shoulder. The pain persisted, and seemed to be worsening each day. It was most severe at night and in the mornings, and gradually lessened during the day. As I was having trouble sleeping, and concentrating on work, I finally went to an urgent care facility one morning, convinced I had a tumor in my shoulder.

At the clinic they took x-rays of my shoulder area. The resulting images revealed a normal shoulder. I was sent home with a prescription for Percocet, and was given a referral to an orthopedic surgeon.

As pain relief was my only concern at the time, I immediately filled the prescription, and took a Percocet dose as soon as I got home. Within an hour of taking that pill, I was flat-out on the sofa, feeling woozy and sick. If the doctor had mentioned this stuff could make one feel sick as hell, I didn't recall hearing it. Worse, I could still *feel* the pain, I just didn't **care** about it.

A few hours later, my television repair man showed up. He was returning my TV set, which was all repaired and ready to go. When I answered the door, he looked shocked. *"What's the matter with you?"* He asked. (Evidently I appeared more pale and sickly than I realized.)

I shared with him that I was experiencing extreme pain in one shoulder, and that a doctor had prescribed Percocet, which seemed to be making me sick. I also told him I was scheduled to see an orthopedic surgeon soon.

The repairman shook his head and said *"That's nuts. You don't need drugs or an orthopedic guy, you need a chiropractor."*

"A Kyro-what?" I asked? I'd never heard of the term before.

He explained that chiropractors helped people with pain – in a non-invasive away, and without drugs. He then said *"What have you got to lose? You can always go back to the drugs and the cutters."*

My **Inner Voice** spoke out: *"If the Percocet drug made me this sick, what will the next guy will recommend? This chiropractor thing has to be worth trying. "*

So I scheduled an appointment with the local chiropractor, the same one that the insightful repairman had recommended.

My appointment with the chiropractor was a couple of days later. The doctor's office was serene and calming, not at all like the other doctor offices I'd experienced. *"Hmmm, we're off to a good start,"* I thought.

The chiropractor himself was a very modest fellow. He started off by taking neck and spinal x-rays. The images were available during that same appointment. When he called me into another room where the x-rays were posted on the light board, I saw images of a person's neck on the light box. On the wall were large illustrated views of normal spines.

I immediately noticed on the x-rays that the little flanges that are on the back of each vertebrae were rotated over to the right in the neck area. It was actually kind of gross – like someone had rotated the bones on a plastic skeleton. I asked *"Who's x-ray is that?!"*

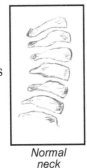
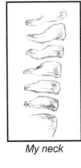
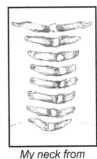

Normal neck | My neck | My neck from the back

He replied, *"That is yours."* Suddenly, I felt ill. All I could assume was that I'd be disabled for life.

The doctor said, *"Don't worry. This is rather extreme, but we can get you straightened out (no pun intended) with a number of adjustments over several weeks."*

"What's an adjustment?" I asked. He explained that my neck muscles were essentially pulling the vertebrae out of proper alignment on the spine. In addition to the rotation, when viewed from the side, my neck had become more or less straight instead of exhibiting the normal soft curvature of a healthy neck. These out-of-place neck vertebrae had caused nerves in my neck to become pinched, and thus the pain in my shoulder. The neck muscles were seized up, and not relaxing as they normally would, so they were essentially holding this improper alignment. The *muscle memory* needed to be corrected/restored.

The doctor further explained that he would manually manipulate my spine, and help the muscles remember their normal state. He also told me that I might hear a sound during this adjustment, and that the sound was normal. Joints typically accumulate pockets of trapped air, and those air pockets can make a sound when they are released. *"Uhm, okay,"* I thought. (This was already a lot to absorb.)

I laid down on my back on the adjustment table. The doctor stood at the top of the table, by my head, and cradled my head in his hands, gently moving my head left to right and back again. Then, with a swift, though not-painful move, he turned my head more to one side. I heard a string of **loud** popping noises. *"What the **hell** was **that?!**"* I asked. He replied *"That was a whole lot of pressure getting released."*

He helped me to stand up, and then I walked out to the front desk to pay my bill and schedule my next appointment. As I was leaving, the chiropractor informed me that the pain relief would likely only last a few hours after this first adjustment, but would last longer with each successive adjustment. I just stared blankly at him. *"Huh?"* I thought. I was still in shock from hearing the popping sounds.

It wasn't until I had walked all the way to my car that I realized the shoulder pain was indeed *gone!* And, I could move my neck normally again. It was incredible. That's a very weird thing – to live in pain for a period of time, and not immediately realize that the pain has subsided.

And, just as the chiropractor predicted, the pain began to return that evening. I went back to this doctor for the additional adjustments, over the course of about 3 weeks. After that, my neck held its own. I have more chiropractor stories to come, but this was how my journey with alternative health options began.

My takeaways: The location of the symptom is not necessarily the location of the problem. Also, drugs are band-aids, they typically have little to do with solving the actual problem. Had I kept that appointment at the orthopedic surgeon, it would have no doubt led to more expensive tests and doctor visits at best, and most likely plenty of prescription medications. As it was, I following my inner guidance, saved a lot of money, and got my health back.

Beyond feeling better and saving time/money, I had discoverd a new map, with new roads to travel. One by one, these pathways became apparent to me, as I opened up to seeing them.

Your Thyroid Function is Fine
No, It's Not

As a teen and young adult I was fatigued much of the time. By the time I was in my 30's, I had needed a nap after school or work since my college days. I would be so exhausted by late afternoon that I could barely function. If I pushed myself through it, and didn't take a nap, I became cranky and frustrated. I slept soundly at night, though almost too soundly. It was more like a coma, and it wasn't unusual for me to sleep 10 or more hours on weekend nights. On top of that, I felt cold much of the time. Wearing sweaters when temperatures were in the 60's/70's wasn't unusual for me.

Many years into this, I learned that these were typical symptoms of low thyroid function. A friend suggested that I have a hair analysis done, as she'd had good experience with such tests in the past. (Good experience as in getting to the bottom of strange symptoms.) I ordered the hair analysis, and was told my test results pointed to low thyroid function. The test results page contained a recommendation that I see a doctor and have blood tests done, including a thyroid panel.

So, I trotted off to my doctor at the time, told him about my symptoms, and requested thyroid tests. He ordered the blood work, and guess what? Everything came back normal. In fact, he said *"I haven't seen blood test results like this since school. Your numbers are **textbook**."*

Well, okay then. At this point I felt embarrassed, and confused. The doctor had looked at me like I was imagining things, yet

I knew something wasn't right. I finally rationalized how I felt, assuming that it must just be normal for me to feel tired much of the time. And so, I went on with my napping, sweater-wearing routine.

A few years later, I moved to a new city, found new friendships and consequently a new recommendation for a wellness chiropractor. I scheduled an appointment with this doctor, as by now chiropractic adjustments were part of my routine maintenance plan. Upon arrival at the office, I was asked to fill out the new patient questionnaire, which was quite extensive. The questions covered everything from my daily routine, diet, supplements taken, health history, exercise, etc. It took well over an hour to complete.

At the time, I felt a bit put off by what seemed like *a lot* of questions, and I decided not to sign up for the doctor's wellness health plan. His office called me later, and told me that they at least wanted to give me their conclusion regarding the results of my intake survey. The office nurse stated that all signs pointed to my having low thyroid function. They suggested that I see an MD, and have blood work performed, including thyroid tests.

"This again?" I thought we already went down this road?

I made my way to a new doctor in this new town, and explained the situation. This guy ordered a full thyroid panel, along with some other tests. The bill to my insurance was over $800 (and this was 20+ years ago), so we were evidently doing some extensive screening.

I was given the results of these tests at an office visit soon after. The new doctor told me everything was just fine with my test results. No thyroid dysfunction was present. When I reiterated my symptoms, and talked about what I'd read on thyroid function, he gave me a condescending look … it was a look that said *"you need prozac or something."* I left and never went back.

I was back to square one, and my napping/sweater routine.

More years passed, and I moved again. In my new location I received a very strong recommendation for a local chiropractor. Still having my routine maintenance adjustments done several times a year, I made an appointment with this guy. At my first visit to his office, the take-in nurse asked me if I had any questions or issues that I wanted to talk to the doctor about. *"Huh?"* I asked? She told me that the doctor was a general wellness doctor and could help with a variety of health issues.

Back to this again. *For the love of* ......

I mentioned the tiredness and chills that I generally felt and left it at that. (I wasn't about to go Round 3 of the bloodwork-came-back-normal routine.) The doctor came in, and I found him to be a very amiable, not in the least bit arrogant or condescending, so I felt immediately at ease.

He did an entire evaluation using applied kinesiology (AK), asking questions along the way. I'd heard about AK on a Wayne Dyer special, and had read about it in the book *Power vs Force* by David R. Hawkins. While the concept sounded fascinating, I had never seen anyone actually use it. It was interesting stuff, though that's about as much as I could say about it at the time. The premise is that your body **knows** what is true and supportive of health, you just need to ask the appropriate true/false questions and have some sort of measurement device for obtaining the answer.

This new chiropractor completed his exam, and then said *"Your ovaries are showing signs of some hormonal shifts, but what's really showing up is a struggling thyroid."*

At that point I burst into tears, telling him that he was the **third** alternative healthcare person to tell me this, but that I could not get any help. All of my blood work aways came back normal.

He said *"Don't worry, we're going to help you. And once the thyroid situation improves, I expect the female hormones to re-balance, as the thyroid is like the command center for many other things."*

He went on to explain that the human body is wonderfully designed to re-balance and heal itself. It typically can deal with any given single issue nicely. But when multiple issues are going on simultaneously, the body often struggles to find it's balance again. His job, the chiropractor said, was to help a patient's body find that equilibrium again so it could do it's own healing.

Inner Voice: *"OMG! … I believe he may actually be able to help me!"*

The doctor did an adjustment, which was even more gentle than the previous adjustments I'd experienced. He also suggested an acupressure point to massage each day, one that specifically related to thyroid. Lastly, he suggested some dietary changes, and sent me home with 2 thyroid-specific supplements.

I must say, that even though I felt very comfortable with this doctor, I had little confidence that anything noteworthy would change. I already had a kitchen cabinet *full* of supplements that I'd found on the internet … none of them seemed to change a thing. But I tried his supplements anyways, along with the dietary changes and massaging the suggested acupressure point.

Long story made short, within 30 days I *STOPPED NEEDING NAPS!* I put that it all caps, and bold, as it is indeed scream-worthy. My entire adult life up until that point I'd felt tired much of the time. All the sudden, I had *energy* to get through the day. And I stopped feeling cold all the time. It was extraordinary. Truly life-changing.

My takeaways: First, blood work as a diagnostic tool is over-rated in my book. We seem to have a cultural obsession with hypodermic needles, but that's a soapbox topic for a different book. Truth is truth, and there is more than one road that leads to it. I now know that many books have been published on the limitations of thyroid test results, how they can be mis-applied, or even be flat-out wrong. Oddly, most of these books don't seem to get read by mainstream doctors.

Sticky Tears, Dry Eyes, and Ancestry
Treating Symptoms Instead of Causes

Several years ago, I started having trouble with recurring styes on my left eyelid. My tears had become thick and sticky, causing some of the glands along the eye lid to become clogged and subsequently infected. Styes are the result of blocked tear glands, which then become inflamed, swollen, and infected. After experiencing several of these painful and unsightly things, I made an appointment with the eye doctor.

My eye doctor told me that this was a common condition that comes with aging. He called it *meibomian disorder*. He instructed me to start applying warm compresses to my eyes, twice a day, to help thin the thickening tears. When I asked how long I should do this, he stated that I would be doing this for the rest of my life, as there was no known resolution for this problem.

Inner Voice: *"Here we go again. Isn't this just treating the symptom? What about the cause?"*

I dutifully did as I was told, and started applying the warm compresses twice a day. After several weeks, it became evident that the compresses did nothing, and changed nothing. The styes continued to develop. The compresses felt kind of nice, but taking the time to do them twice a day was a real pita in an already jammed-packed schedule.

A few months later, I had an appointments with my now tried-and-true chiropractor. Since he'd helped with a number of other miscellaneous health issues, not the least of which was my thyroid function, I decided to run the sticky tears problem by him. I doubted he'd have input on something like this, but figured it was worth a try. He thought about my question for a moment, then the following conversation took place:

Dr: *Do you drink alcohol?*

Me: *Uhm, yeah.*

Dr: *Do you get a "feel good lift" after the first sip or two?*

Me: *Uhm, yeah … doesn't everybody?*

Dr. *Only some people get a real noticeable "happy" feeling right away.*

Me: *Oh.*

Dr. *What is your ancestry like?*

Me: *One half Irish/Scottish, and the rest Pennsylvania/Dutch-Mutt.*

Dr: *Interesting. There is a hormone called PGE1, it's known as a "feel good" hormone. Some nationalities are predisposed to a deficiency in this hormone. Those ancestries include the Irish, Native American, Scandinavian, and some others. Alcohol consumption can force the brain to manufacture some of this hormone, but the body can only produce so much. It's even hypothesized by some researchers that this may play a part in the fact that some cultures have a higher incidence of alcoholism, i.e. people deficient in PGE1 are simply trying to get that "feel good" of PGE1 expression.*

*"**And**, he said, PGE1 deficiency is also associated with dry-eye syndrome … the sticky tears!"*

Me: *Holy crap!! That's wild – I've **never** heard of this before.*

Dr: *The good news is that there is a supplement known as GLA, found in Black Currant Seed Oil. This supplement converts to PGE1 in the body. And it should help your tears/eyes.*

I started taking the GLA that day, and within weeks the sticky tear problem ***went away***.

Many months later I had a checkup at the eye doctor, and told him about this solution. He did a check of my eyes, and said that *"Yes indeed, the inflammation associated with meibomian disorder seemed to be gone."* He did ask what supplement I was taking. While this doctor at least asked what had solved the problem, he didn't seem particularly moved by the resolution of what was to be a *lifelong condition.*

My takeaway: There are extraordinary solutions out there ... ones we will never hear about from many supposed experts. For reasons unknown to me, many experts don't even seem interested in learning anything new.

So often we are told that this or that condition is part of aging and therefore inevitable. But is that always so? Or do we simply believe it because experts say it?

Skin Spots and Black Salve
Down the Escharotics Rabbit Hole

About 20 years ago, I started using a black salve (an escharotic) to treat skin spots and cancers. I decided to try this after seeing the magic a similar product had performed on a horse that had a sarcoid growth. For more details on that story, jump ahead and check out the chapter titled *"Andre and That Thing Over His Eye"* *in the HORSES section.*

As a person with fair skin, I have enjoyed my share of trips to dermatologists. These visits nearly always result in the cutting off or freezing of the latest skin find. Several trips a year to the dermatologist became an expensive undertaking over time (not just in dollars, but in time spent.)

When I did my initial research on the black salves, I discovered many amazing testimonials about people using them to treat various types of skin lesions, including potential melanomas. (Note: my research occurred well before the heavy censorship era, back when search engines results reflected a variety of sources, and not just *officially sanctioned* ones.)

The salve I used was based on bloodroot, an ancient Chinese herb that has been used for a variety of skin conditions for centuries. I won't go into the history here, but suffice to say there is lengthy documentation on its use. A number of books have been written on the topic, and I have one referenced at the end of this book.

I found hundreds of testimonials from people who had been using this salve for years, and these people had virtually eliminated time and money spent at a dermatologists office.

The salve worked on me much like the salve for the horse did. It appears to kill bad cells, while leaving healthy skin intact. The body then recognizes this dead entity, creates new skin, and gradually pushes out the foreign body in the healing process. This involves an inflammatory response, so the area generally becomes reddened and looks worse before it looks better. All of this being completely normal for the process.

After purchasing a small jar of this black salve, I tried it on a couple of skin spots. One spot was likely an AK (actinic keratosis, generally considered pre-cancerous) and the other was a small, dark mole that had recently changed, potentially signaling a melanoma. Both spots *reacted*, meaning there was a mild burning sensation that lasted for a few hours.

I left the salve on overnight, with a light bandage on top to keep it from coming off while I was sleeping. The next morning, I washed off the now-dried product. Both areas had reddened slightly, and the spots were yellowish, as if they had been burned. Over the course of the next 1 to 2 weeks, the *bad* skin areas became like scabs, and eventually fell off, leaving healthy new pink skin behind. The scab where the mole was actually left a small divot, as if the mole went deeper into the skin. Over several months, the area filled in and the skin became flat again.

I began using the salve any time I found a suspect area. Sometimes there would be a reaction, and I would let the process take it's course. Other times, nothing happened, which told me the spot did not involve problem cells, or perhaps was something that wasn't affected by the salve.

Sometimes the burning sensation was very brief. Other times, it was more significant and for a longer length of time. In the latter scenarios, the healing process took longer, and in those cases often there would be the divot or indentation in the skin when the scab finally fell off. Over time though, the divot always filled in and became smooth skin again.

When I mentioned the use of this salve to a dermatologist, I was met with the expected reaction. (Picture stern, disapproving look and language.) As of the writing of this book, I've now been using this product for over 20 years, with near 100% success, So suffice to say I care little about the judgmental stares. I've saved $1,000's over the years in doctor's costs. Not to mention time spent in doctor's offices. Plus, it occurs to me that freezing and cutting seem to be less than ideal approaches when something much more targeted is available. How does a doctor with a scalpel know visually exactly where the bad cells end and the good cells begin?

This product has become much tougher to find in recent years, again, due to governmental crackdowns on many alternative modalities. At one point in the early 2000's, the fda actually raided the main manufacturer of this product and confiscated all of the inventory. The business owner was targeted mercilessly. One might ask: just what would justify such a *huge* reaction to a simple *salve*, one that had centuries of history to it? (In recent years I have come to my own conclusions.)

After a couple of years, the salve became available again, through other sources. Fortunately it doesn't take much salve to treat an area, so one small container lasts for many years.

Several years after I started using black salve, I began to notice that many of the websites and forums praising this product, with the corresponding stories of success, had disappeared. Increasingly, all I could find were sites reporting the salve as quackery and labeling it as downright dangerous. I continued to use the salve, though I said little about it to friends or doctors. I mean, the FDA, doctors, and others were *really* going after this stuff. And I confess, all negative reports planted a tiny amount of doubt in my mind. I began to question my *Inner Voice*.

Then, *2020-2021 happened*. For two years I watched, dumbstruck, as simple/safe treatments were censored and banned. Even talk about Vitamin D was mostly silenced. It was then that I *knew*. Not only were the authorities and experts *not* worried about the safety of the black salve product, *they knew it worked*, or they wouldn't have tried so hard to obliterate it out of existence!

There are some very interesting videos out there featuring Greg Caton ... the guy who helped bring this ancient black salve formulation to the rest of us. Greg Caton has since passed (in 2019), but fortunately some of his insightful interviews remain. Greg also published several books, one of them about black salves (see Resources at the end of this book).

My takeaways: There *are* cures for skin cancer and other various growths. I'm certain of that now. As a number of comedians and journalists have wryly commented on mainstream medicine, *"There is no money in curing cancer, so you won't see it happen. The money is in keeping you alive **with** cancer."*

HORSES

Going Against the (Trainer) Grain
Blown Tendons, and other Collateral Damage

I once owned a lovely young thoroughbred gelding, purchased from a race horse breeder in Kentucky. I had planned to train and ride this horse in the sport of dressage. The horse's name was Unicycler, which friends of mine soon shortened to Cy.

I purchased Cy when he was 7 years old. He hadn't been ridden in years, as he had suffered a tendon injury while training to be a race horse. And after 3+ years of R&R, he was more than ready to get back to some sort of work. As he could no longer be a race horse due to limitations of the old injury, I got him for a bargain price.

Cy was a beautiful chestnut horse, with magnificent movement and a fiery spirit. He was a *looker*, a horse that turned heads, which is a quality one wants to have in a show horse.

Jim, the horse's breeder and former owner, told me before I purchased Cy that the front leg tendon injury had not only ended Cy's racing career, but the recuperation time spent in a stall had nearly made the horse lose his equine mind. The standard protocol for such an injury was complete stall rest (as in no exercise) for a period of weeks or even months. This was the therapeutic approach that had been applied to Cy.

Cy was smart, and very energetic, so being stuck in a 12'x12' box for an extended period of time had predictable consequences. The therapeutic process nearly broke him mentally. When the horse finally got out of his stall, he had to be sedated, just so his handlers could safely deal with him. Jim was a true horse lover, and I could tell that he felt terrible about all of this. Jim's stories about the first few weeks of getting Cy back out of his stall were horrific. It involved tranquilizing the horse, then a minimum of two handlers to get the horse safely out of his stall and into a small paddock where Cy could start to move around again.

I promised Jim that I would give Cy the best home I could provide. I would exercise him and/or make sure that he got freedom time in a turnout area daily. Dressage would not be nearly the physical stress of racing, so we all felt good about Cy's future and his potential.

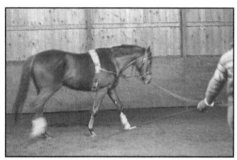

Once I got Cy transported home to Ohio and began working with him, his true talents started to show. He really was a beautiful mover. What's more, he seemed to *like* to work. (Probably the result of being bred for a job.) He learned everything so quickly that I ultimately decided to invest time and money with a local trainer in order to maximize our progress.

Cy was to be stabled at the trainer's facility. During the first month of training he would be ridden exclusively by the trainer. I would later begin weekly lessons on him, learning what he had already learned in the training process.

The trainer called each week in the first couple of weeks to report in, and had nice remarks about Cy's progress. Then, sometime around the third week, she called and reported a problem. She told me that Cy had re-injured his front tendon and would require complete stall rest for a minimum of 6 weeks. (The trainer's veterinarian had been out to the stable, made his diagnosis, the treatment had been prescribed. Case closed.)

I was in shock, how could this be? The type of work she was doing with Cy wasn't considered stressful on a horse's legs. The footing in their arena *was* deeper than what Cy was accustomed to, but still. It was such a sudden occurrence, that I couldn't accept what I was being told, and my **Inner Voice** nudged me to seek out more information.

I called Jim (Cy's former owner), and shared the situation with him. He was kind enough to give his input. Direct and to the point, he said that the horse was likely adjusting to the new, deeper footing, and that the trainer should back off a bit, but *keep the horse moving/working*. (I should mention that *Jim* was also a *people surgeon* in his day job. As in, a very successful medical professional. So he knew *something* about how pieces-parts worked.) And somehow this sounded like a saner response than the immediate *lock him up* approach.

At this point, I decided to go to the trainer's stable and check out the situation myself. When I got there, I found my horse, sullen and sulking in the corner of his stall, with one front leg heavily bandaged – from above the knee all the way down to his foot. He looked like the victim of some tragic accident. *"WTH?!"* I thought.

I went into the stall, and unwrapped his leg, and examined it carefully. I discovered what was *maybe* some slight heat midway down the tendon, but it was really difficult to tell. Certainly not the crisis situation that I'd been alerted to. I took Cy out of the stall, and led him down the aisle. He appeared to be rock solid and sound. So, I got out my saddle, tacked him up, and proceeded out to the arena. There, I mounted up and walked him around the perimeter of the arena. Again, he seems solid and sound. Next we trotted, with the same results. Rock solid, with no sign of lameness At that point I took him back to the barn, unsaddled him, and put him back in his stall, sans-bandages of course.

I then drove home, all the while composing the conversation that I planned to have with the trainer once I got home.

But by then it was too late. When I arrived home, I was greeted by a scathing message on the phone voice recorder. I won't go into details, but suffice to say, the message was quite unpleasant.

At that point, I called the trainer back, and attempted to explain Jim's thoughts on this, that the *backoff and ride lightly for a few days* seemed worth a try ... that I would take full responsibility for any negative outcome from using this approach. The trainer literally screamed at me, and informed me that I was ruining my horse. There would be no discussion, as she had *years* of experience and knew what she was talking about. (an *expert*)

By this point, I was fuming. There was no way I was going to let them destroy my horse's mental state, even if he did end up with a compromised gait. I called around, found a local boarding stable with an open stall, and put a deposit on the stall. Next, I called a trailer service and made arrangements to have my horse transported out of the trainer's barn the next day.

Once I got Cy to the new boarding facility, I proceeded Jim's suggestedapproach. I rode Cy that same day. And every day after that. We took it easy for a couple of weeks, per Jim's instructions, and then just kept on going. A few months later, I took my *ruined* horse to his first schooling show, where we won the blue ribbon in our first ever dressage class. The former trainer was at this show ... I know this as I saw her students there ... though she never approached me. No *"nice to see you, I'm glad your horse is okay,"* no apologies. Nada. Crickets. My horse and I went on to compete at several local shows that summer, and we did very well.

My takeaway: Experts seldom admit they were wrong, much less apologize. In the heat of the moment, *experts* are somewhat prone to being *extremely* attached to their expertise. Which is fine, unless the other person happens to have an inner guidance system pointing another direction. I think this is how fireworks displays were born.

Cy – Ruined, Again?
X-Rays and the Bigger Picture

My beautiful (*though apparently now ruined*) Cy was doing very well in the sport of dressage. We found a new trainer who brought us along swiftly. In just over a year, Cy and I were working two levels of advancement higher than our first ribbon-winning event. (Dressage is a sport of progressive levels of difficulty.) I have to admit, it was an egoic endeavor for me at this point. When Cy and I trained some of the more difficult maneuvers, people would often stop to watch and admire our session. Riding Cy was like a great dance partnership.

Then one day, I took Cy out for a ride, and something felt off. He wasn't exactly lame, just not himself. His strides were shorter than normal, and he lacked his usual drive to move forward. I noticed it again the next day, and the next.

By this point in time I had a great deal of time and money invested into my horse and our sport, so several days of this odd gait situation warranted a trip to a well-known equine lameness expert. The clinic I chose was renowned regionally, as they diagnosed/treated lamenesses in many racing and show horses.

The veterinarian found nothing obviously wrong on a cursory examination, and soon focused intently on Cy's race-training past. The doctor decided to take x-rays on both of Cy's lower front legs and feet. The top veterinarian on staff evaluated these films. Soon, I was given the rather grim report: Cy had two floating bone chips in one foot. These were not a new injury, and the veterinary surmised that these bone fragments had been there since Cy's younger racing days.

My head started spinning. *"If these bone chips have been there for years, why do you think they are **suddenly** a problem?"* I asked

The doctor felt that these bone chips had started to cause inflammation, for reasons unknown. My gut turned, as it made no sense. Again, I asked, *"But why all the sudden? He's been off the track and working well for years."* The vet just shrugged off my question, and said this was the only possible cause of Cy's shortened strides.

Next, the doctor gave his prognosis. Cy's training and showing days were over. I would have to cold-hose his front foot a couple of times a day, to help relieve the inflammation. I was also to give him anti-inflammatory medications, to help relieve the pain. After that, a lifelong maintenance of this condition would be required.

I felt heartbroken that day. After trailering my horse back to the boarding stable, I sat in the aisle outside his stall and cried. All of the time invested, the money, the work, the long hours, only to have his/our career ended like this. Bad news is one thing, but *all of this felt "wrong" at another level.* Bone chips ... really? Then why did my horse seem off on **both** front legs?

For the next several weeks, I cold-hosed Cy's front feet as instructed. I rode him lightly to keep him exercised. And though Cy was receiving the pain medication, he did not seem to improve. If anything, he appeared to be getting worse.

One evening, I arrived at the stable after work and proceeded to brush and saddle-up my horse. I always tacked Cy up in his stall, as the barn was a busy place in the evenings. As I went to lead him out of the stall, he balked. When I finally got him to move forward, I discovered that my poor horse was **dead lame ...** on **all four feet!** Every step seemed like agony for him ... and he didn't want to move at all.

I looked down at his feet, and they had been freshly trimmed, with his shoes reset. So I knew the farrier had been there that day. Of course, I immediately assumed that my horse's feet had been trimmed too short, or had been pinched by poorly placed horseshoe nails.

As luck would have it, right at that time the farrier was packing up his truck, preparing to leave for the day. I lead Cy down the aisle, hoping to catch the guy ... one slow, sorry step at a time.

I said *"Steve, **what** in the **hell** has happened to my horse?!"* The farrier replied, *"Oh good, you are here. I was just getting ready to leave you a long note."*

Steve proceeded to explain that Cy had a ***really serious*** case of *thrush,* and that I needed to get a vet out to the barn asap. "*I buried a hoof pick in the cleft of each of his frogs (in the feet), and never hit bottom,*" Steve said. It's really, really bad. This has likely been coming on for months. You probably didn't see it, as the typical oozing from the frog isn't present.

Thrush is a common infection of a horse's feet. Typically there is a foul odor present and a black, sticky ooze coming from the frog area (circled area on illustration). In Cy's case, the infection had spread inward, so wasn't immediately obvious. It is typically caused by dampness. So, drying out the stall and surroundings is the most critical part of treatment.

And what had I been doing for the last several weeks? I'd been keeping Cy's feet damp ... while the thrush problem got worse and worse. All thanks to a vet that never bothered to look for something like an atypical presentation of a common problem.

And, thanks to my ***not*** listening more closely to my ***Inner Voice.***

The regular barn vet came out, and prescribed oral antibiotics along with a regime of packing and wrapping Cy's feet with drawing salves and topical antibiotics. After many weeks, the infection started to clear, and Cy started to feel like himself

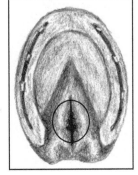

again. He returned to completely normal movement, with not a sign of lameness whatsoever. (Bone chips be damned.)

My Takeaway: Confirmation bias, and in-attentional blindness, are difficult concepts to fathom. We all do these things, at least a little bit. Confirmation bias occurs when we think we know something, and then only look at information that confirms that thing. In-attentional blindness is focusing so intently on one thing that we become blind to other possibilities. All other input that could lead to another conclusion becomes invisible. In my experience, becoming *expert* at something increases the likelihood of conclusions led by confirmation bias. I don't know if egos play a part here, but that seems worthy of exploration. In the bigger picture, I've found that I now become suspicious of any expert that is too certain of anything, especially if they come to their conclusions super-speedy-quick!

Andre and The Missing Gait
Chiropractors for Horses?! Who Knew?

My newly-purchased horse, Andre, arrived at the stable from out-of-state via a horse transport service. He walked off the trailer solidly, inspecting his surroundings, and looked no worse for the wear after his long road trip. A beautiful gelding, with a can-do spirit, he quickly settled into his new environment over the coming days.

For the first week in his new home, Andre just enjoyed some R&R time, and getting to know his new pasture buddies. The following week I started working with him, doing light training on a lunge line. I quickly discovered that he knew his commands, and lunged easily, however I could not get him to canter. All he would do is walk and trot, both of which were smooth, energetic, and with no sign of lameness. He just simply refused to do his third gait, a canter.

After a week or so of attempts to see his third gait, I tried free lunging him – turning him loose in the arena and simply encouraging him to move forward. Even with the full freedom of an arena, he refused to canter. All attempts so shoo him forward just resulted in a faster and faster trot. Then, two of us humans got into the arena with him, and tried shouting and chasing him. He found this quite exciting, and got a bit silly, but would still only proceed a fast trot.

I started observing him when he was turned out in pasture with the other horses, and noticed the same behavior. Even when the all other horses took off as a herd in a gallop, Andre just went after them at a fast trot. He never broke into a canter.

It was very odd. Neither the stable owner nor I had ever observed anything quite like this. I kept working with him for several weeks, and started to wonder if I'd have to re-sell him as a trail horse, absent one gait. Showing wasn't going to be an option without a canter!

About a month or so later, the stable had a visit from an *equine chiropractor*. And while I'd become a big fan of chiropractors for myself, the idea of an chiropractor for a horse didn't quite compute. However, several other horse owners at the stable swore by this equine chiropractor's *magic*, so I decided to ask the gentleman work on my older horse, Baron. As Baron could be a cranky horse, I was curious to see how this would unfold.

The equine chiropractor was one fascinating guy: very cowboy-esque, with a black belt in karate, and lots of talk about *energy work*. He spoke about the energy of the horse, and what happens when it gets blocked. Admittedly, I had little idea what all that meant. But since so many people at the stable said their horse's moved better after this *guy did his magic,* I thought my old horse deserved his very own chiropractic adjustment.

The equine chiropractor then went on to perform an adjustment on Baron. The process lasted about 10 to 15 minutes. He started at Baron's head and neck area, and worked his way along Baron's spine to the tail area. It looked like the guy was making a fist with one hand, and using his other hand to hit the fist (like a hammer on a mallet) at various spots on Baron's spine. It's a little hard to explain, and was weird to watch. I was told to not touch the lead line, or attempt to hold Baron's head in place, or I would screw up the energetic adjustment. I had no idea what any of that meant.

When the process was done, Baron dropped his head and neck, looking very relaxed and quite content. This stance was unusual for Baron, as he typically held his head high, as his normal state was on full alert much of the time.

After seeing Baron's reaction to the adjustment, I asked the chiropractor if he had time to look at Andre too. He said that he did have extra time. So, I put Andre into the aisle cross ties, and the chiropractor observed him for a moment. *"I don't like his stance ... he's all camped-out behind,"* said the chiropractor.

I had no idea what *camped-out* meant.

The chiropractor then proceeded to work on Andrea for about 10 to 15 minutes. When he was done, he said *"Let's put him on the lunge line ... I want to see him canter."*

That instruction led to the following exchange:

Me: *Well, uhm ... he doesn't canter.*

Chiro: *What do you mean he doesn't canter?*

Me: *We've never seen him canter, or been able to get him into a canter. Ever. Even in pasture. He just trots, faster and faster.*

Chiro: *Well, he'll canter now. Let's go.*

So, I got the lunge line out, and into the arena we went. I walked with Andrea to the middle of the arena, and proceeded to feed the lunge line as Andre moved out.

Before Andre had reached the end of the line length, he calmly **walked** right into a canter! It was one of the most beautiful walk-canter transitions I'd ever seen. He then proceeded to canter around and around, as if it was the only gait he knew.

Chiro: *Now send him the other way.*

So, I did.

And the same thing happened. Andre picked up the other canter lead, from a walk. Again, around and around he went.

The stable owner who had witnessed all this, and I were speechless. How is it possible that 10 to 15 minutes of *energy work* could fix something so profound? Andre cantered from that day forward, and the missing gait was permanently restored.

 **My takeaways:** I would never have even thought to consider an alternative approach to this missing gait situation had the chiropractor not happened to visit the stable that day. Hell, I was actually considering selling the horse! And who would expect such a *miracle* to occur after 10 to 15 minutes of *energy therapy*?! Moments of magic and grace show up at the most unexpected times, and are often delivered in quite unusual packaging. I think being open to possibilities is key to taking advantage of these opportunities.

Andre and That Thing Over His Eye
Black Salve Saves the Day

With a canter installed, I was now working with Andre 2.0. He was a lovely mover, with nice conformation. A very noble and beautiful horse. At this point, I thought we were good-to-go on the dressage career.

Within the first few months though, Andre developed what appeared to be a large wart on one of his upper eyelids. It seemed to be getting larger by the day, so when an area veterinarian was visiting the stable for another horse, I asked him to look at Andre's eye.

The doctor immediately identified the growth was a *sarcoid* tumor. He went on to explain how sarcoids are not cancerous, but that they can and often do spread. He recommended surgery, to be followed by high-tech injections around the surgical site which would prevent any remaining growth from spreading. (Note: This veterinarian had recently opened a surgical center, which is probably just a coincidence.)

As I prepared to schedule the surgery, just by chance (or grace?) I ended up in phone conversation with another veterinarian who frequented our stable for routine care visits. I told her about the sarcoid situation and the impending surgery. Her response was immediate, and pronounced: *"What?? Joe actually wants to cut into that thing?!"*

I was a little taken aback by her emphatic response, and asked what concerned her so much. She proceeded to inform me that surgical removal of sarcoids can cause them to spread even faster, and so it's tricky, even with the high-tech shots, to keep that from happening. She didn't want to second-guess the first veterinarian, but thought I should know more, and do more homework, before making the surgical decision.

Then she continued on, *"Look, there is a new product available. It's a topical salve that is supposed to treat sarcoids, and not harm healthy tissue. I haven't tried it with any clients, but I'll sell it to you at cost if you want to try it. It's worth a shot, and you can always move up to surgery if it doesn't work."*

Well, that logic made perfect sense to both me and my inner guidance, so I went ahead and purchased the salve.

The instructions for the salve were quite simple. Apply it to the growth, once a day, for four days in a row. Then leave the area alone. Pretty easy, at least in theory. It turns out that the location of the growth can become an issue when it comes to applying the salve to a 1,000+ pound animal.

I started applying the salve the day it arrived. Days one and two went by with no issues. By day three however, Andre seemed a little finicky about my touching the area, and the skin around the sarcoid was looking a bit inflamed. He finally let me apply the salve on his eyelid. He shook his head a bit, though that's all.

By day four, Andre seemed *much more* reluctant to have me touch the area above his eye. I had to tie him in his stall to apply the salve. After that, he shook his head violently several times and stamped his feet for several minutes, before settling down again. (I was really glad that there wasn't going to be a day five of treatment involved.) After he settled down, I turned him out to pasture with his friends, and left him alone for the next several days.

When I next checked on him, his upper eyelid had become quite swollen, and the skin around the growth was very red. The tumor itself looked more like a scab now, and was raised.

Each day thereafter the eyelid area changed: The swelling of the eyelid started to go down, and the area of redness around the growth started to shrink. The dead tumor itself seemed to be getting *pushed out* and each day the scab got higher. By day ten, it looked like Andre had the root of a small tree growing out of his upper eyelid! A few days later, the dead thing fell off, leaving healthy pink skin behind. The growth never returned or spread.

My Takeaways: Astonishment. Pure astonishment. I started to research this salve, and others like it, and then began using it on my own skin. I've virtually replaced visits to a dermatologist with a similar product. (I wrote about this in the ME section.)

There are many web sites out there now attacking these escharotic products, which is a clear sign to me that these salves have value and do indeed work.

Seeing the extent to which powerful interests went to suppress easy/effective treatments in 2020-2021 has led me to a new health research tool: If the fda and cdc are trying to vilify and/ or shut down a treatment, that is a clear sign to me that the treatment has validity, and quite possibly is extremely helpful. I'm not even trying to be funny here. I actually use the degree of official attacks as a measurement tool for how well an alternative therapy is likely to work. (Attacks mean that big money is generally getting directed somewhere, and as usual, actual healthcare suffers.)

Baron The Lame Horse
Experts and (More) Confirmation Bias

A few years later, Andre had been sold, and I was still pursuing dreams of glory in the tremendously expen$ive sport of dressage with my remaining horse, Baron.

While Baron didn't have the greatest conformation for dressage, he did have a tremendous heart, and was very smart. So, we actually made progress, even winning a few ribbons and trophies at shows.

One day, preparing for a training ride, I saddled Baron. As I walked him into the arena he seemed quite lame on one back leg. The limp was very noticeable, so I unsaddled him and put him outside in his small turnout area. I proceeded to check him over, and could find no obvious heat or injury to his foot or leg. So, I decided to let him rest for several days and see if the situation improved.

After several days it appeared that Baron had not improved. At that point I made the decision to have him seen at a well-know veterinary clinic that specialized in equine lameness.

Upon arrival at the clinic, I was asked to lead Baron at a walk and trot on the outside pavement. Within minutes the lameness expert said *"I believe we are dealing with hock arthritis. Let's get some x-rays of that hock."*

I brought Baron into the clinic, and they proceeded with taking the x-ray pictures of the hock area on the problem leg. After the films were developed, the main veterinarian came out of a back room, followed by another veterinarian and two veterinary technicians. The group of us stood and listened as the lameness expert proclaimed, *"Yes, we are indeed dealing with hock arthritis."*

The doctor pointed to the x-ray now posted on a vertical back-lit board. He took a grease pencil and drew arrows on either side of the hock joint – the arrows pointed to an area between two slab-like bones. He went on to explain that as horses age, the space between those two bones lessens, eventually becoming a bone-on-bone situation. Thus the inflammation and the pain.

My **Inner Voice** inspired me to speak up, and I said *"Baron seems awfully lame and on just one leg. Are you sure this is arthritis? Wouldn't he have arthritis in both hocks? This came on so suddenly."*

The doctor assured me that this was a normal presentation of hock arthritis. He seemed very sure of himself, and of course, he was the expert in the room.

The same doctor went on to say that there was good news in all this. According to him, the natural process with hock arthritis is for the two slab-like bones to eventually fuse together. Once that fusion occurs, the horse actually loses very little range of motion, and becomes free of pain.

"What we want to do here," he said, *" is to encourage this inflammatory process so that the bones do indeed fuse. You do that by keeping him working/moving. He'll seem better some days than others, as that's how arthritis works. Just make sure to keep him moving and working."* The vet prescribed oral joint supplements, and also intra-muscular drug injections, to help with joints/arthritis so Baron could stay working through this process.

I attempted to follow this prescribed path, but most days Baron could only accomplish a walk. He was far too lame to trot or canter. After a few weeks, I called the vet and informed him of the situation. The vet said *"This is normal, just keep him moving."*

I began to dread going to the barn, as watching Baron limp made me feel physically ill. Then, one day, after saddling up, I attempted to get on him. That day Baron nearly collapsed behind.

He had become full-out, 3-legged lame. He could barely put weight on the hind leg.

In tears, I put Baron back in the stable, and unsaddled him. I then proceeded to have a *come to Jesus* moment in my head. My reality had become crystal clear. Not only was I chasing an impossible dream with a horse not even built for the mission, I had neither the time nor the funds to continue pursuing this sport. I was making my horse and myself miserable with the quest. And deep down, when I really thought about it and was honest with myself, I wasn't all *that* interested in the sport anymore anyways.

The very next day I called it *quits,* and began selling all of my show-related tack and clothing. I left Baron out in pasture, and didn't attempt to ride him or work him in anyway. He and I had officially retired from the sport.

At the time, my personal life was also at a crossroads. Around that time I decided to sell my condo and move out west. Baron went with me and we both relocated to Arizona, where we adjusted nicely.

After some time in the sunshine and beautiful surroundings, Baron appeared to be walking soundly in his turnout area, so I decided to try riding him around the property. He did just fine at a walk, and as the days went on we began to slowly explore the surrounding trails. These were some of the most enjoyable rides we'd ever had together. No work, no stress, just the quiet and magnificent scenery.

Later, about 6 months into our Arizona adventure, I arrived at the ranch to find a veterinarian on site. The doctor had a mobile x-ray unit and was taking pictures of another horse's legs for a pre-purchase exam. I asked the doctor if he would mind taking a few images of Baron's hock. I shared the arthritis background story, along with the symptoms that ended Baron's show career. While Baron and I would never return to training and showing,

I *was* curious about the status of the hock arthritis. At least to some extent, this lameness was in part responsible for igniting some major shifts in my life.

The vet said *"Sure. Have the previous clinic send us the original films so I have something to compare these to in the evaluation."*

When I got home, I called the original clinic in Ohio and made the arrangements for the earlier x-rays to be sent to the Arizona veterinarian.

The following week, I received a call from the AZ vet, and the following exchange took place:

Dr: *Hello Kelli, this is Dr. Tom.*

Me: *Oh Hi! Did you receive the x-rays from Ohio yet?*

Dr: *Yes, they arrived.*

Me: *Well, how does the hock look in comparison to those films?*

Dr: <<*silence for a moment*>> *Well ... the hock looks fine. But did they say anything to you about the broken fibula?*

Me: *The broken...,* **wait ...** ***what?!***

Dr: *There is an obvious fracture of the fibula bone on these Ohio x-rays. My receptionist saw it as soon as she pulled the films from the envelope.*

Me: *May I come to your office right now and see for myself?*

Dr: S*ure.*

I proceeded to speed over to the veterinarian's office, fully convinced that the wrong x-rays had been sent from the Ohio clinic.

When I got to Dr. Tom's office, he showed me the film on the light board. There, right in front of me, was an x-ray image displaying a label with my name and Baron's name in the upper right

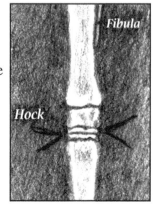

hand corner. And there were the grease pencil arrows pointing to the hock joint. Several inches away, was a *clean break in the fibula bone*. I was dumbstruck, it was impossible to believe.

I recalled the original Ohio clinic visit. There had been **five** of us who had looked at this x-ray image the previous year. Because our attention was so fully focus on the hock (as we were *following the expert*), **none** of us had seen that break just several inches away.

To say that I felt stunned would be a dramatic understatement. Dr. Tom said that such a break was rare, but not unheard of. It was usually the result of trauma, such as a kick from another horse in pasture situations. He went on to say that while the fibula is not a weight-bearing bone in a horse, this kind of injury could be quite painful.

"What would be the treatment recommendation for this type of injury?" I asked.

"Rest." He said. *"Certainly no riding or training."*

My Takeaway: Ironically, the expert in this case wasn't really *wrong* with his diagnosis. Baron did have hock arthritis as the x-rays revealed. It's just that the *diagnosis* wasn't the cause of the *pain*. And at some level, I knew Baron's lameness wasn't due to arthritis when the first vet made that diagnosis. But I had been too afraid to question the man too much, as he had such a large presence and reputation.

Baron's lameness story is a tough one for me. To this day I am sad that I put my horse through such pain, convinced by an expert that I was helping him. To the best of my awareness and ability, I'll never let **that** sort of scenario happen again. An *Inner Voice* asking questions is doing so for good reason.

DOGS

Macintosh the P.C. (Personal Canine)
When Meds That Help Become Meds That Hurt

My dear old mutt, Macintosh (Mac), was over 12 years old and really looking every bit *The Senior.* He had become very skinny, as for the last year it had been difficult to get him to eat much of anything. His teeth were okay, he just seemed to have little interest in food, even in people food.

That year, my other dog Beauty was called to cross over the Rainbow Bridge. While Mac didn't seem to miss her much (truth be told he wasn't all that fond of her), I noticed a major energy deficit apparent in the house. Both Mac and I just seemed a bit lost.

In the hopes of enlivening our home, I adopted a new second dog. This young, boisterous male was a large doberman named Capone. And boy oh boy, did this addition ever super-charge our atmosphere.

Mac and Capone hit it off day one, and they became fast friends. Mac really seemed to love Capone, where he had simply tolerated Beauty. Mac even ate a little bit better, seeming to be encouraged by watching his buddy eat.

One day the following year, I was letting Mac and Capone outside via the back patio door when Capone spotted a rabbit farther out in the yard. Ever the *hunter*, Capone launched off the deck like a rocket, powering into poor old Mac and rolling the old dog down four or five wooden deck steps. Mac stood up with a WTH? look on this graying face.

A few hours later, I noticed that Mac seemed short of breath. He was breathing rapidly, only taking in short sips of air, and panting, like he was struggling to breath. I immediately took him to my vet, where they rushed him to the back of the clinic for x-rays. One of the doctors came out shortly thereafter and asked *"Kelli, was he hit by a car??" "What?! NO!"* I said. *"But Capone did crash into him earlier today."*

"I don't think that would be enough to do it," she said. *"Do what?"* I asked. She then stated that **both** of Macs lungs had collapsed. The doctors had inserted needles into Mac's chest cavity to release some of the air pressure so that the lungs would re-inflate. They had relieved some of the pressure, but Mac would need to go to a 24-hour emergency clinic and be monitored through the night.

"Holy crap!" I thought!!

I gathered up my poor old dog a short while later and headed outside towards my car for the emergency clinic trip. The main veterinarian, who had become a friend over the years, caught me on my way out of the building. He said *"Kelli, if they want to do surgery at the emergency clinic, and crack open Mac's chest, don't let them do that. Mac is nearly 13 years old, and too old to be put through a major surgery like that." "Agreed completely,"* I said, and off we went.

Mac was admitted for overnight care at the emergency clinic, and all I could do was wait for a phone call. The next morning the clinic called to tell me that Mac was still alive, but they'd had to insert needles two different times overnight to release more pressure so Mac's lungs would stay inflated. They wanted me to come to the clinic and discuss the *options.*

When I got to the clinic, a doctor came out to talk with me. He introduced himself as a surgeon. He explained that Mac had several *bullae* or weak spots on the walls of his lungs, and it was these spots that were allowing the air to escape. The surgeon wanted to do surgery, i.e. crack open Mac's chest, and *fix* the weakened spots. I looked at the guy like he was crazy. *"No way. My dog is nearly 13, very skinny and weak, I'm not putting him through that kind of surgery."*

The surgeon was obviously pissed. He leaned in, sternly telling me that if I didn't have this surgery done, Mac would be dead within a month. *"Then I'm taking him home to die."* I said. *"Just let me pay my bill. And give me back my frigging dog."* (The expert in this case was just a flat-out jerk. I can't even go with good intentions on this one.)

I took Mac home, and prepared myself mentally. The next time I saw him with distressed breathing, I was going to rush him to my own vet for that *final* trip.

During the time all of this fun was occurring, I ran out of Rimadyl, which was the arthritis medicine that Mac had taken the last several years. I didn't get the prescription refilled, as I figured he only had a few days left anyways.

About 2 days went by as I waited and watched. One evening when I was in the kitchen cooking, Mac showed up all bright-eyed with tail-wagging. I looked at him and asked *"Sweet Pea ... are you **hungry**?"* He started dancing around and wagging his tail even more. *"How odd,"* I thought ... I'd been practically begging him to eat for the last year, and he had shown no interest in food. As I mentioned earlier, he was quite skinny, as he barely ate anything.

I made up a small dish of food and put it down for him. He proceeded to wolf all of it down in no time, and then begged for more. This skin and bones dog, who'd had no appetite for over a year and was supposed to die soon, was suddenly ***ravenous***.

He continued to eat well from that point forward. It was days, maybe even weeks, before I made the connection: *The **Rimadyl** had been making him **sick**!*

To shorten a much longer story: The dog that was supposed to die soon ended up living for another 3+ years. He ate well every day to the end, and gained back enough weight to look normal again. I never again gave him Rimadyl, or any other arthritis medication.

And whether the Rimadyl had anything to do with the lung condition, I'll never know. What I do know is that after I stopped giving him that drug, he became a healthy, vibrant pet again. Sure, he had more gray hairs as time went on, but he was definitely happy and energetic.

My Takeaways: Experts seem A-okay with fixing one thing and breaking something else in the process. I've lost track of how many linear decisions have been made, just by the experts in my life, that end up causing unintended, sometimes horrific, consequences. Worse, many experts don't even care that this is the case! They seem to be single-mindedly focused on what they want to *fix*, all else be damned. Perhaps all the other consequences just becomes new/fun things to fix?

Capone the Hunter
Surgery and Drugs: That's All You've Got?

When my 10+ year old Doberman Capone developed a slight limp in one of his hind legs, I took him to the vet for evaluation.

X-rays were taken, and a small mass was found in Capone's hock joint area. The vet said that these types of masses were typically malignant, and that a biopsy would be required to confirm.

I asked what would be the recommended treatment if indeed cancer was confirmed, and the vet stated that leg amputation was nearly always recommended in these cases. That sounded horrifying to me, especially on a large/senior dog, so I said that I would decide what to do after the biopsy results came in. *"Oh no,"* the vet said, *"the amputation is done at the time of biopsy."* Somehow the process of sticking in a needle in the mass most often resulted in a need to amputate anyways. *Dear Lord.*

To say that my inner guidance reacted strongly to this news and suggested *therapy* would be an understatement. Cutting the back leg off of a large dog, a senior dog at that, seemed incredibly barbaric. Adding to this information, I did some additional research and discovered that once a dog is symptomatic with such a cancer, there is a high likelihood that it has already spread. *"So if it's cancer, and has likely already spread, what's the point of amputating a limb?"* I thought.

I continued to do research, investigating alternatives to limb-severing surgery. The running theme of all the sources I found was this: The healthier the body, the better chance of fighting off just about any disease, including cancer.

Knowing that I could never be convinced to go the recommended surgical route, I decided to apply some of the alternative and more holistic therapies I discovered. I then came up with a sort of home recipe for treatment.

First on the list, I switched Capone to a raw food diet, something he loved beyond measure. (I figured what the heck … even if he only has a little time left, at least he'll enjoy eating stuff he loves.) I also added in a number of vitamins and supplements, and did daily Reiki treatments on him. And most of all, I prayed.

To make a long story short, Capone thrived. While he continued with some limp on the hind leg, he never seemed to be struggling with pain or even stressed. Capone continued to chase little critters and beg for his long walks. He lived three more years, which for a large Doberman is something special indeed. He thrived nearly all of that time, walking with me and chasing bunnies right up until just days before he crossed the Rainbow Bridge.

Can I proved that our healthy living approach worked and is responsible for his longevity and vitality? No, I can't. All I can say is that I'm convinced it helped him, based upon the results. I have applied this *customized holistic recipe theory* to myself, and to later pets, with incredible results. Sometimes it takes extra work and effort, however I've saved a ton of time and money which would otherwise have been spent on doctors and prescriptions.

My Takeaways: When a helpful measure *sounds* crazy and barbaric, it probably *is*.

When inner guidance speaks: **Trust. The. Voice.**

Blue and Buglets
The Scorched Earth Approach of Preventatives

Several years ago, I adopted a senior doberman. She was a blue doberman, and didn't answer to the name she came with, so I called her Blue. *(Creative, eh?)*

Blue had a number low-level health issues when she came into my life, so I developed a holistic recipe for her as well. It was focused on good food, lots of exercise, supplements, lots of love, and gratitude for having her in my life. She eventually became healthier and started to thrive.

The first couple of vets I tried were quite cavalier with the prescribing of this or that drug. Shots here, preventatives there, and a prescription medication for dang near everything. My inner guidance kept speaking out, getting louder and louder, finally almost yelling that all of these pharmaceuticals could not possibly be healthy for my dog. So, I started to ask questions, and push back.

Many vets don't like such questions ... not one bit. One has to be prepared to put on some serious armor to head down this questioning road. But I'd had enough experience with *experts* by this point, that I wasn't interested in ignoring my inner guidance any more.

That said, the first year I had Blue, I did acquiesce to several of the vet's recommendations: *routine* shots, monthly heart worm preventative, and monthly flea/tick preventative.

The use of the word *preventatives* here is misleading in my book. Prevention is about doing something that **prevents** something else, with the **implication** it is a healthy action to take. Pet preventatives like heart worm and flea/tick medications are actually poisons. These drugs don't actually **prevent** the pests from getting into the dog, they just kill the little buggers once they've invaded. And most veterinarians are perfectly okay with this. We're routinely promised that these products are *completely safe* for our pets. But if you're like me, and start to dig around for actual data, you'll find out that *safe* is not a word that should be associated with any poisons, including these universally recommended drugs.

So, in an attempt to not completely alienate the vet, I tried to at least space these *preventatives* out, so Blue's body didn't get everything at the same time. (i.e. heart worm preventative on the first of the month, and flea/tick preventative mid-way through the month.)

I also discovered that heart worm preventatives can actually be given every 45 days, so I started giving those at 1.5 month intervals. (*Experts* decided that people would forget and neglect giving the heart worm pills at odd intervals, thus the monthly recommendation. Or maybe it was about money. Probably both.) I still gave Blue the flea/tick stuff monthly, but on a different week from the heart worm pills.

Each time Blue had the flea/tick preventative, she seemed to slide in her health. Diarrhea one time, throwing up another time, general malaise another time. I started to become worried about giving her the pills, so by the end of that fall, I stopped altogether and decided not to give it her any more of these in the future. She was nearly bald, a genetic issue that happens with many blue dobermans, so she was not a great home for fleas anyways. And thanks to the near baldness, I would easily be able to spot any ticks that lodged on her.

About a year went by, and Blue's health improved greatly. I dropped the heart worm pills for the winter, and swore off any more *routine* shots unless absolutely necessary. The next time Blue was due for shots, I ordered titer tests instead. Titer tests reveal the amount of antibody protection that still exists against this or that disease. Often, a booster shot isn't even warranted.

Here's where things start to get interesting. (And keep in mind, the flea/tick pills are considered *monthly* preventatives.)

Over a year later, I was able to do a few November and December deep woods hikes with Blue, as Ohio was having a lovely mild, late fall. It didn't occur to me to check her for ticks, as our hikes were so late in the year. A few days after one of these hikes, I noticed what looked like a thorn embedded in Blue's inner thigh. I tried to pull it out, but it was really stuck. After carefully removing it with tweezers, I put it under a magnifying glass. It was actually a *dead tick*! In November. And by dead, I mean really dead, as in crunchy dead.

"Why was that tick dead?" I thought. Oh well … I moved to other pressing matters and forgot about it. The next month, in December, a similar thing happened around Christmas holiday. I found a tick on Blue, 1-2 days after a hike. The tick was embedded, and again, deader-than-dead.

I had several more instances like this the following winter.

So, for over **two years** after Blue's last dose of flea/tick medicine, *something* was killing any ticks that bit her. Just exactly how long does that *preventative* poison last in a dog's system? And if it was the flea/tick preventative that was responsible for these dead ticks (can't imagine what else it might be), then why in the hell do we need to give it to pets *monthly?*

My Takeaways: I have no answers to the above questions, and am only reporting my personal experience. If you also have questions about our current approach to pet preventatives, I'd suggest seeing the movie *The Dog Doc,* and checking out Dr. Marty Goldstein's books. These resources yield ideas for and have suggestions on *actual* prevention plans that doesn't rely so heavily on pharmaceutical poisons. Dr. Marty Goldstein is sometimes called the Father of Integrative Veterinary Medicine.

Unfortunately, not all veterinaries who self-label as *integrative* are offering alternative solutions. Some of them are just mainstream vets offering boutique and expensive extra services. As is the case in most healthcare decisions ... you have to do some homework and listen to your own inner guidance.

Blue's Neck Pain Protocol
When Science Isn't Science

The first year I had Blue she developed issues with neck pain. Her symptoms were similar to those of a human with a pinched nerve in the neck – turn the wrong way and experience sudden, extreme pain.

Poor Blue would cry in pain when she lifted her head at certain angles. She also had a shortened gait in her front legs. I took her to the veterinarian, who prescribed a 3-week course of Prednisone along with a drug for nerve pain. Blue had several of these episodes in her first year with me, and each time it was a trip to the vet and subsequent prescriptions for Prednisone and pain medications.

It seemed like a lot of drugging, especially when one dose of prednisone turned Blue's pain around completely. This is not an exaggeration. About 6-8 hours after one dose of Prednisone, Blue was doing great and back to completely normal movement.

I remembered being told many years ago, by a holistic vet, that sometimes Prednisone could be used on an *as needed* basis. This of course depended on the circumstances, and it could not be used frequently. It was like ibuprofen for a dog in scenarios like this. I asked the current vet about using this limited drug approach, and she said *"No, a 3-week protocol with tapering is what is prescribed."*

During each of these treatment periods, by week two of the Prednisone Blue was suffering from serious medication side effects. Prednisone can cause excessive thirst and appetite. Blue was drinking *bowls* of water a day, she was ravenously hungry, and was peeing everywhere. She was a very well-behaved dog, and knew that urine smell did not belong inside. She seemed more upset about her accidents than she had been about the neck pain! We were quickly adding *stressed out* to a list of symptoms to deal with.

During the third round of this treatment approach, I called the vet and asked if there was any way to speed up the tapering-off of the Prednisone, as Blue was exhibiting zero signs of pain, and all of the side effects were making both Blue and Kelli miserable. The vet acquiesced slightly, and we got Blue off the medication a few days early.

Three weeks after this third Prednisone treatment cycle, Blue was scheduled for her annual checkup. I took her to the veterinary clinic, where they drew blood for both a thyroid re-check, and for the heart worm test. About a week later, the vet called me with the test results: Blue's thyroid function was down, and I was told to increase Blue's thyroid medication by 50%. That doctor stated that if Blue became hyperactive (which is a symptom of too much thyroid supplementation), I was to notify the clinic office.

"Huh?!" I thought. My dog is *not* gaining weight, and is the *antithesis* of lethargic. (Gaining weight and lethargy are the hallmarks of *low* thyroid function.) I couldn't believe Blue actually *had* lowered thyroid function.

I voiced my concerns to the vet, who proceeded to *double-down* on what the blood work results indicated.

My *Inner Voice* demanded that I investigate further. I then went on a research binge. And guess what I discovered? I found out that a course of Prednisone can skew thyroid results ... *for up to 6 months* after the course of Prednisone is completed!

I called the vet back and asked about the information I had found. Her reply? *"Oh sure, we can leave her at her current dose of thyroid supplement, and then re-check the thyroid test in 6 months."*

Translation: *"We screwed up, though we won't acknowledge that, or apologize, or congratulate* **you** *for finding the information. So lucky you – you get to pay for two thyroid tests this year."* Or something like that.

After this Blue and I moved on to another vet clinic, and then another, before I finally found a match. There **are** tremendous veterinary doctors out there, but sometimes you really have to look to find them, and always ask *lots* of questions.

My Takeaways: Any veterinarian that makes you feel uncomfortable for asking questions, or doesn't accept push-back should be fired, immediately. Some of the younger vets are, unfortunately the worst about this. They have no idea that their education was *sponsored and written by Rockefeller Medicine*, or that entirely different perspectives are often valid. Too many practitioners have been brainwashed to believe that pharmaceuticals are the answer to everything. One way to break from being enslaved by this system is to fight back with quality information.

Blue and Melanoma
Black Salve, Again

This story is the dog version about skin spots and black salve.

Within the first week or two of adopting Blue, I noticed a small growth on the inside of her hind leg. It seemed to be growing quickly. It would also start to bleed, then heal, then bleed again. After several cycles of this bleed and heal routine, I got into research mode. Turns, out, these are telltale signs of a doggie melanoma. I also looked up quite a few images on the internet, and many examples of dog melanoma looked exactly like the growth on Blue's leg.

By now I knew that the only thing a veterinarian would have to offer would be biopsy and surgery, I decided to give my black salve a try on the dog, and see if it did anything.

Fortunately, as the growth was just above her hock area, I was able to apply the salve and then lightly wrap the area to keep Blue from licking it.

Evidently the salve did burn a little bit, as for a few minutes Blue tried to lick the bandage. After that though, she ignored it completely and slept soundly through the night.

The next morning, I removed the wrap and was stunned at what I saw. The raised growth was completely gone – the skin was flat, and what was left was only a flat, black scab-like area. Over the course the next several days, the area became swollen and inflamed. While Blue did not show any sign of pain, I suspect it itched a bit, or felt irritated, as Blue seemed to want to scratch at it and lick the area.

As this was a now-familiar process, I knew that her body was in healing mode and preparing to expunge some dead tissue. The whole process took almost 3 weeks, as the growth ended up being quite deep. Like Andre, a longish scab (dead tumor) gradually emerged and pushed out of her leg. A large divot as left behind, with new healthy skin lining the area. After a number of additional weeks, that area filled in completely with new skin.

As I write this, that salve treatment is over four years behind us, and the skin still looks great. The growth never returned.

No Takeaways here. It's probably obvious that I've become a big fan of black salves and many other alternative therapies.

Final Thoughts

Moving Beyond Experts

Our Health Scare System
The Healthcare War

Everybody has a topic of interest, or perhaps several. Most of the time we don't know where these interests comes from. it seems we're just born with them. Like I was born with a love of horses, dobermans, etc. And for reasons unknown to me, I've always had an interest in health as part of a grander scheme.

Many people don't realize that our culture tends to train us to think of our health in war-like terms. In our early formative years, we are taught that we are **separate** from everything around us, and that there is always some unseen *other* out to get us. Yet the air is rich and full of microscopic organisms that are supportive of life, our life. The same can be said for surfaces, water, the earth, etc. Very few people have ever heard of the microbiome, yet this is the environment in which each of us is immersed every day.

Thanks to a fully materialistic view of our world, we are encouraged to sanitize nearly everything! Humans take a scorched-earth approach and attempt to obliterate all germs. The result being that we end up *destroying all of the helpful organisms* as well.

Ask a lawn care expert how this works. They will tell you that the healthiest lawns are the ones that are fertilized, watered, and not over-mowed. An occasional weed-killer is okay, but most weeds will be kept at bay by a *healthy* lawn. And what do you get if you just rely on weed killers? You end up with a decidedly *unhealthy* lawn, and herbicide-resistant weeds that are even harder to kill.

Does this scenario sound familiar? Think about the history of antibiotics. What happened when doctors started prescribing antibiotics for nearly everything? (The scorched earth – kill 'em all approach.) We ended up with antibiotic-resistant germs, and torched gut bacteria. As it turns out, much of the bacteria in one's gut is *good*, and actually needed for health and digestion. (Of course all of this carnage spawned the probiotics industry, so there's *that*...)

This doesn't mean that washing one's hands is a bad idea. But to become obsessed with it, carry hand sanitizers everywhere, continually sanitizing every surface, well...

The *kill everything so I can survive* strategy seems to be a doomed idea no matter how one views it. Any degree of pulling back the lens on this approach reveals the inevitably outcome. I doubt life for humans or pets will end well if we keep going with this short-sighted (and fear-based) strategy.

The best marketing ever invented is to create or frame a fear, fan the flames of that fear, and then sell the solution to that fear. To a large extent, that's what our health scare system has done.

Having said all this, there is one thing that our healthcare system handles well, and that it trauma care. Rockefeller medicine does really well with part replacements, and putting humpty-dumpty-humans back together after accidents. And sometimes we do need these things! It's pretty amazing stuff – these high-tech fixes.

But when it comes to helping a person stay in balance, stay healthy, our mainstream medical system is that last place I'd turn for advice on this topic. If you want some interesting reading, look up the term *Rockefeller Medicine* and you'll start to understand how we got here. (Short version: it's all about $$$.)

Evolving Faith

As faith is a deeply personal topic, I don't typically talk a lot about that aspect of my journey. I'll just close with some brief general thoughts.

My faith journey has taken me down many roads: exploring different religions, meditations, yoga, rituals, readings, travels, and more. And here is where I am at with it today:

I've found that the surest way to close the door to my inner guidance, is to attempt to figure everything out or develop an intellectual understanding of the dimension of the divine. The greater realms simply cannot be understood by the human mind. For me, being willing to fully accept the state of not knowing is what opens the door to new understandings. And while the experience of the unknown is beyond words, it somewhat paradoxically has a language of sorts, and that language is found in gratitude, trust, and love.

Resources: Books and Movies

For a number of years, and especially since 2019, search engines have pretty much obliterated alternative health site results. So, I'm listing a few of my favorites below. Each on of these resources has played a key role in my health journey.

Books:

Doctoring Data, by Dr. Malcolm Kendrick

You Can Heal Yourself, by Louise Hay

Natural Vision Improvement Kit, by Meir Schneider

Healing Back Pain: The Mind-Body Connection,
     by Dr. John E. Sarno

Black Salve, by Greg Caton

The Nature of Animal Healing, by Dr. Martin Goldstein

Movies:

The Dog Doc Documentary, by Cindy Meehl

1986, The Act, by Andrew J. Wakefield

About the Author

Kelli Swan is both a published author and an artist who specializes in pencil and pen&ink drawings. Educated at the University of Akron in Ohio, she received her BFA, with a minor in mathematics, and Summa Cum Laude honors. Kelli draws her inspiration from a life-long love of animals and nature, along with moments of grace.

Kelli's interests include reading, hiking, swimming, lots of exercise, and time spent with family and friends.